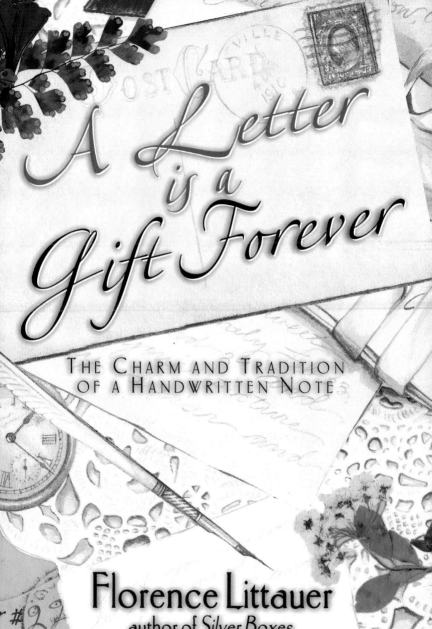

A Letter is a Gift Forever

THE CHARM AND TRADITION OF A HANDWRITTEN NOTE

Florence Littauer

author of *Silver Boxes*

with Tammy Bennett and Rose Sweet

Artwork by Gay Talbott Boassy

A Letter Is a Gift Forever
Text copyright © 2001 by Florence Littauer
Published by Harvest House Publishers
Eugene, Oregon 97402

Library of Congress Cataloging-in-Publication Data
Littauer, Florence, 1928-
A letter is a gift forever/Florence Littauer; artwork by Gay Talbott Boassy.
p. cm.
ISBN: 0-7369-0429-8
1. Letter writing. 2. Interpersonal communication. 1. Talbott Boassy, Gay. II. Title.

PE1483.L58 2001   00-059752
920—dc21

Artwork designs are reproduced under license from © Arts Uniq'® Inc. and may not
be reproduced without permission. For information regarding art prints featured
in this book, please contact:

        Arts Uniq'
        P.O. Box 3085
        Cookeville, TN 38502
        800.223.5020

Design and production by Koechel Peterson & Associates, Minneapolis, Minnesota

Harvest House Publishers has made every effort to trace the ownership of all poems
and quotes. In the event of a question arising from the use of a poem or quote, we
regret any error made and will be pleased to make the necessary correction in future
editions of this book.

Unless otherwise indicated, quotations throughout this book are by Tammy Bennett.

Scripture quotations are taken from the Holy Bible, New International Version®,
Copyright © 1973, 1978, 1984 by the International Bible Society. Used by permission
of Zondervan Publishing House.

Printed in Hong Kong

01 02 03 04 05 06 07 08 09 10 /NG/ 10 9 8 7 6 5 4 3 2 1

Contents

Letters from the Heart

$\mathcal{P}$rogress is always a good thing—or is it?

Will the romance of a ride through the park with a horse and buggy ever be replaced by hoisting oneself into a huge Suburban?

Will a child's excitement over watching ice cream mysteriously form in a tub of rock salt ever be surpassed by an orange Popsicle?

Will a handwritten note on crisp, perfumed vellum ever be equaled by mechanical Email sent to every friend the writer can remember? When the hurried writer ends the message with "I love you all!" does that mean that he really loves me?

Not necessarily so.

A Letter Is a Gift Forever is full of real letters, written by real people on real paper. They appear exactly how they were written, full of love and maybe even spelling mistakes.

This loving collection comes from gracious people who have attended my seminars, and also friends and family members of Rose, Tammy, and myself. It includes a letter from my Scottish grandmother to her mother in Nova Scotia in 1898. She writes of her new home in Massachusetts and describes the rooms I later played in as a child.

Letters–
A family album
of times gone past

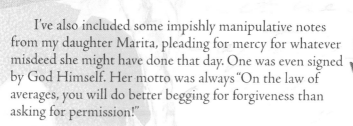

I've also included some impishly manipulative notes from my daughter Marita, pleading for mercy for whatever misdeed she might have done that day. One was even signed by God Himself. Her motto was always "On the law of averages, you will do better begging for forgiveness than asking for permission!"

There are some precious notes from Rose's stepson who wrote to explain why he couldn't say "I love you."

Tammy's husband shares a note he penned to his future mother-in-law just before the wedding, thanking her for raising such a beautiful and competent daughter. This letter alone lifted her spirits and established a loving life-long relationship.

This compilation of letters, filled with both love and humor, will warm your spirit and remind you of how wonderful it is to give and receive the gift of written words.

The next thing most like living one's life over again seems to be a recollection of that life, and to make that recollection as durable as possible by putting it down in writing.

— BENJAMIN FRANKLIN
The Autobiography

A Very Pretty Place

Little did I know when I went to our family reunion in tiny Merrimac, Massachusetts, what a treat was in store for me. My brothers and cousins along with their families stood on the sloping lawn, looking up at my grandmother's house where my mother had lived until she married at the age of 27. My cousin Don asked if he could speak to us. He was from a quiet branch of our talkative family and least likely to address a group loaded with speakers and pastors. What did he have to say?

"I have in my hand an original letter from our grandmother. She wrote it to her mother, our great-grandmother, in 1898." There was a gasp from us all. We had no idea there was any such letter and the aggressive ones of us wondered, "How did he end up with this?"

He continued, "She and grandpa arrived here from Canada with three children, Annie, Sadie, and Katie, who was only six months old."

Katie was my mother! This letter was written when my mother was six months old!

"Our grandparents had just moved into this house that we are looking at today, and she wrote this letter to her mother back in Nova Scotia, reviewing the trip down and giving a description of this house." We all looked up at the white clapboard house that had stood here for 100 years!

Don began to read.

Dear Mamma,

I guess you are all beginning to think I have forgotten all about writing. But I will tell you how it was I did not write before.

I stayed a few days in Brockton and moved here on Tuesday. I have been getting settled ever since.

We had teas with Mrs. Dunehan, the woman Mac boarded with when he came here first. She treated us fine. She is the only woman I have met here yet. So you know it being near the last of the week I left writing until tonight when I would have more to tell you. We are all quite well and I am glad to say I have not got home sick yet and I hope the Lord I will not. The weather has been fearful hot since I came here but while I was in Brockton it was quite cool. We had a thunderstorm here on Friday night. The lightening was very sharp. It is lightening a little tonight but I don't think it will amount to much.

I remembered how afraid my grandma was of thunderstorms—how she had hurried me to the basement one night as claps of thunder seemed to be banging on this very roof.

Well I must say that this is a very pretty place. It is so much like our country. We have a lovely house rented with six rooms: kitchen, dining room, and front room, also a little porch and pantry off the kitchen, and a closet in the dining room on the first floor. Then there are three bedrooms up stairs, and a clothes closet in each room. The rooms are all square for there is an attic above them. The house is pretty. It has a little veranda as you come in the front door and a nice bay window in the front room.

I looked up at the bay window. My mother and father were married standing in the window. I had opened presents sitting in there at my wedding shower. My grandmother, this one writing the letter as a young wife, had been laid in a casket in that window. It was the focal point of the house. You got married there, you celebrated there, and you died there.

There is as much ground attached to it as all that yard of Warren's put together, but it runs farther back. There is a nice lawn in front and side and gardens in the back with apple, peach, and plum trees, also a grapevine and large bed of tame strawberry plants. If God spares us till next summer we will have a fine garden. There is a nice grove in back of the house that we all like to stroll through on Sundays.

How I loved my grandma's gardens. Our family lived in our convenience store that didn't have even a blade of grass out front, only cracked black paving that sprouted up an occasional weed. How I had wanted a real house with lawns and gardens. How as a child I had longed for flowers, any

kind of flowers that you could pick and put in a vase. Grandma's
yard had been the only pretty part of my life. When I visited
she let me smell the roses, eat the fruit off the trees, gather
up the strawberries to make jam, and pop the concord grapes
out of their skins into my mouth. I looked up and there were
the same trees, only bigger, not bearing much fruit because of
neglect. The grape arbor was leaning over having been weighted
down through the years. There were a few wild daisies in
place of the cultivated flower garden Grandma wrote about
in the letter.

> I have a lovely place to hang my clothes. There
> are four posts driven with pieces across the top with
> pegs to string the line on and there is lovely
> green grass beneath it. I was telling Mac if you were
> here, you would be washing the windows and helping
> me get settled.

> I forgot to say that Mac went right to work. We
> got here on Tuesday afternoon and he went to work
> at Judson's Carriage Factory Wednesday morning. Our
> home is about a four minute walk to the shop.

My grandma had been so proud of her husband, Mac,
who had died when I was only two. She would take me for
walks down to Judson's and point out that my grandpa had
become a foreman at the shop and had been a major part of
the transition from carriages to cars. It was hard for me to
imagine that there was a time when people didn't have cars.
Judson's was closed now, an empty building, a hulking symbol
of better days and the price of progress.

Our home is on the main avenue, where the street cars run but it is as far as the church is from your house, so there is no danger of the children getting run over. They have a fine place to play. Annie is very good at amusing little Katie.

Little Katie was my mother. It was hard for me to picture her as a baby.

We get to bed quite early and get up early. Mac goes out to the grove nearly every morning and gets wood while I make breakfast. We have coal but I like to burn wood. It does not make such a heat and we can get as much hardwood as we can burn.

Bye bye,

Your daughter

Florie

This letter was written by
Florence Anne Conrad MacDougall to her
mother, Catherine Anne Murphey Conrad,
in Nova Scotia, Canada, 1898.

"Florie" was the nickname for Florence. I had been named after her, and of all the family, I had a special love for the one who had given me her name. Are you named after anyone in your family? Are you carrying on a legacy? Do you perhaps have some old family letters sitting in the attic? If not, perhaps this reading from my grandma will inspire you to begin to look for some. Older family members are often harboring old missives, photos, and correspondence that may be lost forever if you don't ask. Begin today to search out mementos that will provide a legacy for future generations.

Grandmama Purvis

In all her years Grandmama Purvis only gave me two gifts, both of which hold precious memories. One was an old hand-stitched quilt from her back bedroom. Neither of us knew it would be our last visit together when she handed me the quilt and said, "I just wanted you to have it."

The second gift was quite a surprise. Grandmama grew up reading very little and writing a lot less. Like most little girls in the rural South, she married at the ripe old age of 17 and became a farmer's wife, like her mother.

Life was hard for Grandmama. Over the years she gave birth to seven children, with her first child arriving in 1921 and the last in 1934. During the course of her life she would bury three of her children, a daughter and son killed in separate accidents by drunk drivers, and a baby boy who died of pneumonia. Grandmama taught us all a lot about being a mother.

Grandmama was quick-witted and always set to tell a story. Her lack of formal education made it nearly impossible to sit with pen and paper and write out one of her fascinating stories. Whether she had an audience of one or 21, she loved to sit in her favorite upright recliner, swing her legs over the armrest, and commence to tell a family tale.

In 1980, when she was 76, Grandmama gave me the second present. I had gone to my mailbox one day and found a small envelope addressed to me with her simple cursive handwriting. I'd never received a letter from Grandmama and couldn't imagine what had prompted her to write. In the past I'd noticed little handwritten notes next to her kitchen phone, but had never seen her write a formal letter. Her script appeared painstaking, with the letters short and sharp.

I opened the envelope carefully, reverently, to find a folded piece of paper from a stenographer's pad. There, in her own writing, were Grandmama's words expressing her joy at having just learned from her son, my father, that I was pregnant, and about to make her a Great-Grandmama for the very first time.

I was moved to tears. This woman whom I'd looked up to had always been an icon of strength. I'd admired and respected her from the time I was small. Today she was telling me she was proud of me! I was helping her to give life to another part of her family, another patch in the quilt of her legacy.

After that she and I got together and I taped Grandmama telling some of her stories. She loved seeing herself on

Letters—
A gift to you
reflecting my heart

videotape; she was a star! In her last year I dedicated my first book to Grandmama and invited her to a book signing. She had her hair done, applied a little powder and blush, and put on a new dress. She sat next to me in a rocking chair that seemed to swallow up her now frail frame, and the local paper came and took our picture.

I keep her letter framed and hanging on my wall, along with the photo of her at the farm wearing a wide-brimmed straw hat, dusty field dress, and big smile.

SUBMITTED BY
EVA MARIE EVERSON

A man may write
at any time, if he will set
himself doggedly to it.
—SAMUEL JOHNSON

Lolli & Pop

With the birth of each grandchild, I wrote a simple note to welcome them. To make the note even more personal, I traced around my husband's hand, then mine inside of it. We instructed the parents that as the child grew older and knew who we were, they were to show the child the hands and place his little hand in ours.

Because I didn't want to be called "granny" or "grandma," I came up with fun names for my husband and me. I'd be Lolli and he'd be Pop. When we visit they call out "Lolli and Pop are here!"

POST CARD
April 1, 1994

Dear Austin,
Here are our hands to hug you and hold you.
Thank You God, for Austin and his mommy and da'
We love you lots!
Lolli and Pop

SUBMITTED BY PAT DAMON

Letters—
A grandparent's
method to mail a hug

Letter from the Groom

When Tammy announced that she was getting married, I remember what mixed emotions poured over me. I started having serious doubts about the union that was to take place between my daughter and her fiancé, William Edward Bennett III. They were so young, he was in the military, they would move away, and neither seemed to understand the responsibilities that followed the wedding. And though I pondered these thoughts in my heart, I moved forward towards the date of the wedding. It seemed as though the calendar rushed the hours and days at its own hurried pace, bringing into fruition, all too soon, the plans, hopes, and dreams I had been preparing for. With anxiety, I met the day praying that I would have some kind of assurance that this union would beat the odds and be "a match made in heaven," which every mother desires for her daughter. That assurance I longed for did come, hand delivered, as a letter from my soon-to-be son-in-law just hours before the wedding.

Letters—
The beginning of a
beautiful relationship

October 24, 1981

Dear Mr. and Mrs. Presson,

Things have been hectic but I'd like to let you know how much I appreciate all you have done in the past six months to make the wedding plans go smoother. Of course, without your daughter none of this could be possible, so I thank you for doing a wonderful job raising her. Basically, I just want you to know that I feel I have a wonderful set of in-laws and I consider myself extremely lucky to be able to call myself your son-in-law. Again I'd like to thank you for everything you've done and let you know I love you both very much.

God Bless You,
Edward

My anxieties were put to rest with just one handwritten letter. It wasn't profound, poetic, or persuasive, but it was genuinely personal.

The paper and the envelope have since yellowed with age, but I still treasure the message that Ed sent. His tender thoughts healed the anxieties of my heart. Their marriage has been a delightful 20-year success, presenting us with two exceptional grandchildren and continuing the blessings our son-in-law promised.

How many of us could change our attitude towards our in-laws with some loving words? O, the power of a positive pen!

WRITTEN TO MR. AND MRS. PRESSON
SUBMITTED BY TAMMY BENNETT

The Camp Counselor

Because my mother's motto was "children should be seen and not heard," she sent me off to summer camp when I was a gangly eighth-grader. I remember stomping up the steps to the dormitory for 12-year-olds, where I threw my sleeping bag on one of the cots, shoved my suitcase underneath, and went back outside to take a look around. The church campground was crowded with counselors calling out names as parents kissed their campers good-bye. The air was pungent with pine, and I suddenly felt hungry smelling hot dogs on an open fire. Being here was just fine with me, I thought, because I'd always excelled at sports and I loved outdoor activities. The camp counselors were like big sisters, making sure we had plenty to do and helping us find our way around. As the week passed we played games, swam as much as we wanted, and sang campfire songs. I had so much fun that I never even gave a thought to life back home. Until the sun went down each day.

I longed for my mother's arms around me and her reassuring words that everything would be all right. But night after night, I found myself alone in the dark. Exhausted every night, I'd snuggle into my sleeping bag, curl up on the hard cot, and cry. I tried to forget about my mother's announcement that she was getting divorced for the umteenth time and pretended I came from a normal house like the others. I did all right until the sun went down.

Letters—
Boost the spirit and bring
healing to the soul

I guess my bright and bouncy manner during the day didn't mask the pain that was in my heart. One of the camp counselors named Barb must have seen something in my eyes, from the first day. I remember she had soft, pretty eyes and a sweet smile. It was Barb who brought comfort to my little camper's heart that summer.

After crying myself to sleep the night before, I awoke one morning to find a construction-paper card, which Barb had hand drawn and decorated, at the end of my bunk. On the outside was a colorful crayon rainbow and Barb's perfect printing in purple pen of a verse by Albert Camus:

Suzy

In the midst of winter, I learned that there is in me an invincible summer.

Camus

"In the midst of winter I learned that there is in me an invincible summer."

How appropriate! I was feeling bleak, like winter had overtaken my heart, but Barb's card showed me that the warmth of summer is always available to us. She continued with her own words of encouragement:

"I believe in the sun even when it is not shining.
I believe in love, even when not feeling it.
I believe in God, even when He is silent.

Sometimes when I cry I feel as though it has just
rained leaving me fresh, able to continue once again. . .
Love takes time, tears, sadness, loneliness and all the
other beautiful experiences of life.

Suzy. . . . when I first met you there was something
in your eyes that told me "here is one of those gentle
people who radiate beauty simply by living. Maybe it
will help just to know. . .

I care.
Barb

Barb had seen past my pretense and tried to dispel my discouragement. I will never forget sitting up in my cot that crisp, cool morning and being blanketed in the warmth of her letter. Barb made me feel special with her words that mattered the most: *I care.*

I've kept that card with me into adult life, where it continues to cheer me up on days when I feel down. It's a little more yellow with the years, and the rainbow isn't as bright as it was that summer, but Barb's message still shines.

Have you noticed someone in your life whose smile might be masking some sorrow? Maybe you could help bring the warmth of summer to their winter of worry by simply saying, "I care."

SUBMITTED BY SUZY RYAN

Someone of Obvious Caliber!

I was a middle child with a quiet temperament. In my large family of ten, I often felt lost. My mom and dad were highly educated and worked hard to keep all their children in private schools. I learned about life from listening in on my parents. I wanted to share my dreams of being in the air force, of being a doctor or research scientist with them, but fearing ridicule, I kept quiet. I know they loved me, I could feel it at times, but they just did not know how to show it emotionally. All I ever wanted to do was please them, but I didn't quite know how.

School was one way I could get their attention and approval. Although I wasn't as vocal as my brothers and sisters, I knew I was smart and I loved to bring home straight "A" report cards. The only trouble was that all the other kids in our family got A's too! It was not very often that I got any special attention, until the year I got the letter.

I was a high school student who'd been assigned a semester of independent study in biology. A teacher was only present during this semester to encourage or advise—not to teach. Science was one of my passions, and I was excited that I could use anything in the lab for my project. The excitement soon faded, as I became frustrated with my bacterial project. I was so discouraged about struggling again on my own and had almost no self-confidence in my efforts. We were supposed to write a paper at the end of our project describing our work and final conclusions. When the semester came to a close, I still hadn't been able to answer the original question I'd posed about the bacterium I'd investigated. I felt stupid. It was obvious I would never be a doctor!

The teacher suggested I send a copy of my paper to the authors of the science textbook from which I'd worked and pose my question to them. I appreciated the advice but knew for sure that they would never answer a high-school girl. Instead I was shocked when I got the reply letter that read (in part):

University of Colorado   April 1971

Dear Miss Sweet,

Your letter was a breath of fresh air for those of us who have been working in the second year of the BSCS (Biological Sciences Curriculum Study). I received tremendous pride and warmth from knowing that the course could attract a student of your obvious caliber...Your questions are...pertinent and...appropriate. The answers you seek are at the frontier of our knowledge about genetics.

I wouldn't like to try to answer your questions. Your hypotheses are every bit as good as mine and the current literature...Thank you for a delightful experience. We appreciate your letter.

Patrick E. Balch
Staff Consultant

I was thrilled! Imagine! Me…at the frontier of genetics! I had "scientific evidence" now that I was good, that maybe I could be something significant.

I never did become a scientist. Eventually I had six children and a marriage that ended in divorce. I saved the original letter in an album for many years because it meant so much to me. It often got me through tough times. One year one of my children emptied the album of all its contents and the letter was lost! For a long time I was heartbroken. During this time in my life, though, I finally turned to God for the guidance I had always needed, and He was faithful to give it, helping me work through my painful past. I learned that my yearning to do something in the scientific world was rooted in my love for humanity and my desire to help people. How blessed I have been to be able to continue in my own ways to help many people in my family, my community, and my church!

It had been a long time since I'd seen that letter, and I thought I didn't need it anymore. Now that I am at peace about who I am, one of my kids just recently found the letter! I was as excited as if I had just found a lost diamond…a BIG diamond! In a way I'm just like that letter; God preserved me even when I thought I was lost. I think finding that letter today is His signature on my life.

I know I will never be without encouragement and guidance. As dear as that letter is to my heart, it pales in comparison to the knowledge that my heavenly Father loves me and sees me as "someone of obvious caliber"!

WRITTEN TO SERENA SWEET ON APRIL 26, 1971
SUBMITTED BY ROSE SWEET

It's Never Too Late

$\mathcal{I}$ stood at the curb outside the airport terminal, ignoring the chattering crowd and the wet winter street. As I breathed in the crisp, cool air I realized that in the next two days I would travel back 40 years!

I'd flown up from Palm Springs to a grade-school reunion-planning meeting in Sacramento and was waiting for my girlfriend, Terri, to pick me up. When she drove her car to the curb, I hopped in, threw my bags in the back, and buckled up. "Where are we having the meeting?" I asked, not really waiting for an answer. "I hope they have food. *I'm starved!*"

Terri replied, "Tommy Ahern's house. Do you remember him?"

I froze. I hadn't seen Tommy since grade school, but I dreamed about him over the years. I had hurt him deeply and had never forgotten. It wasn't a big thing, but I had been eight years old and it was the first time I ever felt ashamed of myself.

It was 1959 and our third-grade teacher, Mrs. Blackburn, was reading to us that day in class. We all sat in our seats, quiet and obedient, the boys in their salt and pepper pants and we in our starched sailor midis. I loved school and I already knew then that I wanted to be a teacher someday.

Someone tapped me on the shoulder and handed me a note. I was shocked because notes were expressly forbidden, and if we were caught, we would be sent to the principal's office. Still, I was curious and opened the letter and read it.

Dear Rosey,
I love you. Please meet me
after school by the bike racks.

Tommy Ahern

I had never really paid that much attention to Tommy. He was nice enough, but my mind was on books, not little boys. I thought he was dumb because he didn't spell my name correctly, it was not Rosey. It was R-O-S-I-E…how stupid could someone be!! I was a little afraid that Mrs. Blackburn might see me with the letter, so I decided to raise my hand immediately and turn it in to her. That way, she would know that I was not a willing partner in Tommy's classroom crime! She would be proud of me and appreciate me. All I thought about was me.

She stopped her story, walked down the aisle, took the letter, and headed back to the front of the class. I saw her silently read the note and assumed she would stick it in her pocket. Instead, she stopped and announced to the whole class, "Tommy Ahern has written Rosie Sweet a letter," and she proceeded to read the letter to the class. All of a sudden I felt sick to my stomach. I didn't want to get Tommy in trouble. I just wanted to clear my own name. I didn't know she would humiliate him…I didn't want her to do *that*! Poor Tommy. I turned to look at him, three rows over and two seats back. His face was bright red, and he sat still in his chair, looking straight ahead, while everyone else but me giggled. I wanted desperately to catch his attention and give him a look of apology.

She continued in a condescending tone, "This is very bad behavior and, Tommy, you will be punished. You must stay after school. Come see me after class." I looked over at him again. *Oh-please-look-at-me*, I thought. I wanted him to see the

Letters—
Passing notes in class seems to be a gift
we are all born with. Getting away with it
is a skill to be developed.

sorrow in my eyes and to somehow let him know I did not
mean to hurt him. I'll never forget his face when he did turn
and look. It was pure hatred. He glared at me so hard I
thought I would shrivel up and blow away. No one had ever
looked at me that way before.

Tommy successfully avoided me for the next five years
until we graduated and went off to separate schools. I was
too young to know how to approach him and make amends,
so I tried to forget how uncomfortable I felt whenever I saw
him. Over the years, thoughts of him would pop up in my
dreams. My counselor told me I probably dreamed of Tommy
whenever I was feeling ashamed because current events might
trigger emotions of my first-time experience. A few years ago,
I thought about searching him out on the Internet to make
an adult apology, but I could not find him.

Now we were minutes away from his house and I was
about to come face-to-face with this middle-aged man I still
called "Tommy." I wondered if he remembered.

I was actually a little grateful that I had the opportunity
to say what I've always wanted to say for more then 40 years.
How many of us ever get the chance? When he opened the
door I saw thinning hair, a smiling face, and twinkling eyes!

Man does not live by words alone,
but he sometimes has to eat them.

—ADLAI STEVENSON

Eyes that once held daggers for me were now clear and bright! Whew! Maybe he had forgotten after all! Others from the group were there and we all laughed and hugged and exclaimed how "no one had changed." Then I quickly grabbed Tommy aside and said, "I have wanted to talk to you for 40 years about something..." Before I could finish my sentence he asked, "The LETTER?"

We both burst out laughing. "Yes! Oh, Tom..." He interrupted. Leaning toward me he confided in a serious tone, "I have never been so humiliated in all my life." He paused as if to relive the moment. "It was horrible."

I reached out, grabbed his arm and blurted, "Oh, Tom I know! I'm so, so sorry!" I led him into the kitchen. "Let's talk," I said. I began my heartfelt confession that was many years overdue. He was warm and kind, laughing a little, but listening intently as I sought forgiveness for my self-centered behavior so long ago. I was a little teary-eyed and felt eight years old again as I finally got to say what had been in my heart. We hugged and laughed and then started reminiscing about the rest of our classmates. The shame of the past melted away as two little kids in adult bodies rekindled a friendship.

When I left that day, I told him I had become a writer. "I've always wanted to write the story of your letter, Tom, but I guess I couldn't because the ending hadn't happened yet. Today it did. Thank you."

Sometimes we have thoughts from the past that keep tapping us on the shoulder. Is it time for you to make a call or write a letter? It's never too late to say: I'm sorry.

SUBMITTED BY ROSE SWEET

Mikey Likes Me!

Stepmoms are expected to rock the cradle, but not rock the boat. When I became a stepmother, I found that emotions run high whenever broken families are blended in a new marriage. As a stepparent, I was expected to take good care of another woman's child, but to never try to be his mother. Who wouldn't want to "mother" my new stepson, two-year-old, blonde, brown-eyed Mikey, who could already name all four Ninja turtles and loved to pick dandelions for me!

I'd always wanted to be a mother, having been the oldest of eight children and Junior Mom all my life. I love kids and kids love me. "Mother" is a title I looked forward to from the time I saw Mom bring home that first little blanketed bundle. Sadly, in my previous marriage, I had been unable to have children. That marriage eventually ended in divorce.

I'd tried and failed in my quest for both marriage and motherhood, but I bounced back in a few years and began dreaming of a family to call my own. I found that dream with my husband, Tom. With him the family seemed ready-made. Mikey, his son, was adorable. I think I was as much in love with him as I was with his Dad, and I couldn't wait to teach him all the things Moms teach—sharing, loving, playing. There was just one hitch—his mother's anger.

Even though I had not known Tom or his ex-wife when they divorced, I understood how Mikey's mom could still be fearful that I would try to take her place. I tried to be her friend, but she wanted no part of me.

What really hurt is that the warm affection Mikey displayed at home with me stopped when his mother was present.

What was my role in this child's life? Should I expect love but not loyalty? I knew the stepparenting books said not to rush or force any loving relationship with stepchildren, but it was too late. Mikey had jumped up into my arms from the first time we met and, without trying to take anyone's place, I had indeed become another "mother" to him. At night I would tuck him in and tell him he wasn't the son of my body, but he was the son of my heart. Then I would kiss him and say, "Good night, I love you." I knew he loved me, but unlike most children, he never said, "I love you" back.

Would I go through life never hearing him tell me he loved me? I constantly wrestled with my own emotional security.

When I confided my fears to my husband, he wisely advised me to be content in the knowledge of Mikey's love, whether I heard him tell me or not. I knew he was right and decided to stop seeking assurance of Mikey's love as validation for who I was. Coming back to my basic identity as God's daughter, I remembered I didn't really need to have a title, or a role, or even an "I love you." So I let go.

Letters—
Children bring joy into our lives
and laughter into our hearts

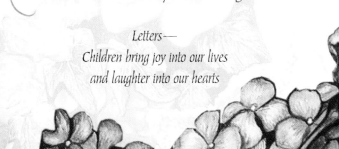

A week or so later, Mikey came up to me and said, "Rose, go look in your room!" Curious, I went in and immediately found his little printed letters on my bed. I picked them up and read them through tear-filled eyes:

1. I'm glad your (sic) my stepmom because your (sic) funny and you love me and I love you.

2. I'm glad that you do a lot of nice things for me and really loveing (sic) things.

3. I'm glad that you think I'm nice and you think I'm sharing.

Later, Tom told me he'd asked Mikey if he wanted to write down some things he liked about me. I got more than I could ask for, and when I finally looked up, I saw Mikey standing in the doorway, shy, but intently watching my face.

"Come here, you!" I smiled affectionately through my tears, put the letters down, and thrust my arms out wide. He grinned and came over and gave me the biggest hug I think he'd ever given me. I didn't want to let go. After that, whenever I tuck him in, or whenever I tell him I love him, he always says, "I love you, too."

For whatever reason, maybe your children have trouble expressing their feelings. Sometimes writing thoughts down on paper frees us to say them in person.

SUBMITTED BY ROSE SWEET

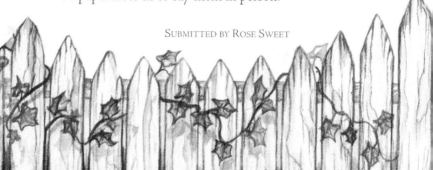

Marita's Letters

*D*id you ever have a child who was a con-artist? One who knew how to twist a sentence so you'd say yes to something you opposed? One who would flatter you richly before coming in for the kill? One who found profuse apologies easier than perfect behavior? Our daughter, Marita, from the time she could talk and work her eyes (an expression she created to explain her ability to lure people with a provocative look) has had an innate ability to charm the socks off of any unsuspecting person. When we had company, my oldest daughter, Lauren, and I would be in the kitchen while Marita would be entertaining the guests. She told stories about what happened in school that I'm sure never happened. She could embellish any tale to brighten up a routine experience, and she never let the truth stand in the way of a good story.

Not only was Marita creative in the art of conversation, but she learned that when she might be caught and punished for some misdeed, it was best to write a letter and place it where I would find it. That way if I were going to get upset over the bad news, she wouldn't be around until I'd had time to calm down. She knew that I thought everything she did was adorable and that her father was much more into discipline. She would address the notes of apology to me.

Letters—
Children have a way of manipulating
themselves into our hearts

When she was 12 years old, the church was sponsoring a Jesus Hike. Teens marched through the streets, sang hymns, and gave out evangelism booklets. Marita was too young, but she wanted to march with the teens.

We had already said, "No," so she decided on a different tactic: make the note come from God! Surely we could not turn Him down! She wrote the note on a round piece of paper, put a string through it and tacked the string to the top of the door frame leading into our bedroom. When Fred and I came home later that evening, she was sound asleep—or at least pretending to be. When we went to our room, here was the hanging note greeting us at eye level.

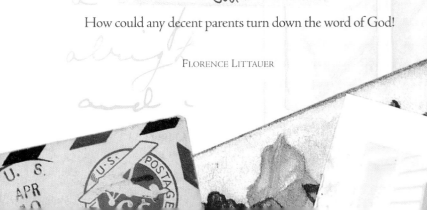

Let Marita go on the Jesus Hike. If you are wondering who is spe talking this is the Lord. I will be with her and Protect her she will be able to work for you saterday and your work will be blessed if you allow her to go

I know you will Let marita go,

God

How could any decent parents turn down the word of God!

FLORENCE LITTAUER

Big Trouble

When Marita did something that she knew would get her into trouble, she would write me a letter of advanced apology. She never spelled out the specifics. In case I'd missed some of the depressing details, there would be no point in bringing them to light.

The following would get an A+ in con-artist school. I found the note, in an envelope, taped to the inside of my closet door.

The envelope read:

> Mom
>
> (Mother)
>
> (Dove) A nickname she used when she feared retribution.
>
> Mother,
>
> I appreciate you being so understanding. I realize I was fully wrong! And that I have been fully wrong quite a lot lately, I'm sorry. Now I know saying I'm sorry just doesn't make it write (sic). However, I feel I should be punished. I also feel that I can keep my self from doing it again with will power + God's help I can over come it! Please accept this and forgive me

like you always have. You have been the best a mother
could be. I know of no better. Now since dad's busy
with his problem's, let's not pester him with ours. We
can solve it ourselves!

I love you, I really do and don't want to hurt you.
I just don't think first. And don't think of how hurt
you'll be. I'm sorry and I love you.

You can take this as my promise never to do this
again in the near future.

Love in Christ, (and other ways)

Rete

Florence Littauer

Matthew's Letter

*J*ust before Christmas in December of 1997, we received this letter from our then 14-year-old son, Matthew. Now he has never been a very scholarly lad, so when we received something handwritten in an almost-essay form, we sat up and took notice. We knew it had to be about something extremely important to drive him to something resembling schoolwork outside of class. As we began reading the carefully crafted letter, we soon realized that we'd better get on the parkas because we were getting a big snow job!

Dear Dad and Mom,

I want a Flugelhom because I think it is a pleasant lovely toned brass instrument. Any melody just spills out of the bell like a song by Pavarotti. Like the orchestral hom of France the tone is richer than an ancient Persian king. To listen to two or more Flugelhoms together is like listening to a chamber choir of well trained Madrigals. This German single hom adapted in 1809 by a German instrument maker named Flugel is the finest creation since the slide on the trombone. To look at the gorgeous lacquered brass coiled together in such an intricate manner is like looking at strands of shiny necklaces. To know a Flugelhom player is like knowing a Duke or a fine Nobleman.

The valves of this German hom slide up and down the valve slots like shredded Persian silk. The spit valves of this noble instrument let spit out as fine as a faucet with a bad dripping problem, the only difference is that the horn doesn't drip till you make it do that. Yes, the Flugelhorn truly is the master horn of tone, melody, a lovely appearance, and great spit valves.

I must have one for Christmas.

Matt

The whole letter was carefully plotted to fulfill his heart's desire, as he carefully manipulated the sentiments of our hearts. It wasn't by accident that he used lines such as:

"Any melody just spills out of the bell like a song by Pavarotti."

and

"To listen to two or more Flugelhorns together is like listening to a chamber choir of well trained Madrigals."

I enjoy listening to Pavarotti and he knew it, after all I don't know how many times he's complained about having to listen to that particular CD. And as for the Madrigal singers, we had just heard them in concert two nights before and he knew that I was spellbound by their voices.

Then there was the part that read,

"To look at the gorgeous lacquered brass coiled together in such an intricate manner is like looking at strands of shiny necklaces."

What mother isn't entranced by the mere thought of shiny necklaces?

And then, contemplating that he had got our attention, he went in for the kill:

"To know a Flugelhorn player is like knowing a Duke or a fine Nobleman."

He knows very well that both his father and I cherish the thought of him entering into a noble profession in spite of his grades in school, and with this he gave us hope for his future.

In reality I think the letter would have sold us if he would have ended on the Nobleman note, but not Matthew. He went on to say,

"The spit valves of this noble instrument let spit out as fine as a faucet with a bad dripping problem, the only difference is that the horn doesn't drip till you make it do that."

Of course if you'll notice, after he described the spit valve in such a glib manner, I think that he quickly realized what he was saying, and tried to save himself. He knew that I would not like the thought of spit spilling out over my floor, so he quickly added, *"the horn doesn't drip till you make it do that."*

Did you ever want something so bad as a child that you would have gone to almost any extremes to get it? I can remember many times when I worked on manipulating my parents with unforgettable words to achieve the ends to my means.

So are you asking yourselves, "Did he get the horn or not?"

Yes, he got the horn, but not because we were manipulated into it, but because we had purchased it long before he took the initiative to write the letter!

SUBMITTED BY TAMMY BENNETT

Bryan's Letter

Marita's nephew Bryan seems to have inherited her persuasive genes.

$\mathcal{F}$red and I were paying part of our grandson's tuition to a private school when he had a particularly bad year. It was sixth grade and he was not doing his homework or behaving in class. When we heard about this, we suggested to his mother, Lauren, that perhaps it was time for him to leave this expensive school and go to the public school. Lauren discussed this possibility and in response Bryan wrote us this letter that I think should be placed in the con-artist Hall of Fame.

Dear Grammy and Papa,

Over the many years that I have been attending Valley Prep, I have learned much. My grades don't show it. Even though they have started to decrease you have paid for part of the bill all these years. If I hadn't been at that school for all that time my intelligence would not be as high as it is. Thanks to you, I am able to go there and receive an education that would not be possible without you.

It has been brought to my attention that my low grades are pushing you to relinquish the money you are supplying to my education. I understand that my grades are depressing and stopping support is looking like the right thing to do. I am trying very hard to raise them. They are going up, but at a slow pace. The laziness that I possess must be shown no mercy and be

vanquished. I need to drastically change my habits and rearrange my priorities.

All I can give you is my word that I will shape up and hope that you will believe me. By this I hope that you will not stop funding my education at Valley Prep. At that school, I have teachers that care and want me to succeed—which I want to. If you were to stop helping me I would be forced to go to a public school. I don't want that to happen. And if it did before my lifestyle changed, my grades would definitely change. They would go down. Please continue to support me and I will try my hardest.

Bryan

Do you think we could take him out after a letter like that?

FLORENCE LITTAUER

In youth, men are apt to write more wisely than they really know or feel; and the remainder of life may be not idly spent in realizing and convincing themselves of the wisdom which they uttered long ago.

—NATHANIEL HAWTHORNE

Dearest Auntie

*M*y great-aunt Jewel was very near and dear to my heart during my formative years of growing up. Much of who I am is a reflection of her today. So you can imagine when she died and I was only 16 years old, it nearly devastated my young life.

She had passed away on commencement Sunday, and so when the pastor spoke of her untimely death, he spoke in terms of graduation. This was something that I could easily understand since it was a process that I was quite familiar with. When my mind would not allow me to come to terms with death, it did allow me to acknowledge graduation—advancement into heaven. It was as though she was going off to college, the University of Heaven.

I somehow wanted to express to her my loss, but at the same time offer my congratulations to her on a life that we, as Christians, all long for—life eternal with our Savior. I penned these words on a graduation card that was never actually sent, but yet I know my words were whispers sent up to heaven the moment I wrote them.

Dearest Auntie,

Congratulations, you did it! I didn't really understand why you had to go until Pastor Race made it so clear. I can't wait to graduate so I can see you again in your heavenly body without pain.

Remember that you will always be special and precious to me. You and Uncle have always meant the world to me. I promise to take good care of Uncle. I love him just as he loves you, and I love you.

I can't wait to someday be present with you and Jesus, and I want so much to meet your darling mother you told me so much about. I know she must be a beautiful person just as you are. I know that she meant as much to you as you mean to me. I truly love you.

I'm sorry I couldn't bring myself to come in and see your earthly body at the funeral home. Please understand I love you and I couldn't bear to remember you that way.

Were the pearly gates the first things you passed through? Have you walked on the streets of gold that the Bible tells us about? Do you really have a mansion? Is heaven the most wonderful place you've ever been? Heaven sounds so wonderful, I wish I could at least visit you there.

Have you asked Jesus unanswered questions? I think I will make a list to take with me so I don't forget to ask one question that has puzzled me on earth.

I already feel as if it has been years since you've been gone. I'll be there some day with you. I can't wait. Won't it be wonderful to spend eternity together and know that we'll never have to be separated again? I'm thankful for the memories I have, but I'll be happier when we're together once more.

It may seem silly to write you this card, but I know that you're alive and present to be aware of what I'm writing since I can't send this to heaven. I'll write often. I know I need not write but it makes me feel better.

I just thought of something, you really are an angel now, even though you were my angel here on earth. Now you're my angel in heaven. Thank you for always being there to take care of my family and me. If it wasn't for you and Uncle, I don't know what would have happened to Mom, Lisa, and me.

I miss you. You'll always have a special place in my heart. I'll always love you. I promise.

I'll see you at my graduation.

I love and miss you,

Tammy

Sometimes we have to write a letter we know we will never send to relieve the pain or record the joy we feel within our own hearts. Would you feel better if you wrote a letter today?

SUBMITTED BY TAMMY BENNETT

Letters—
There are letters addressed:
"Emotional Healing"
and then rendered to our own heart

Three Simple Words

It was 1958. On my seventh birthday Mom and Dad took me out to lunch, presented me with my first Cinderella watch, and when the waiter had cleared our plates and no one was within earshot, told me the family secret.

They'd decided I was old enough to be told that Dad had been married before he met and married my mother. It was a difficult marriage from the start and ended in divorce. I was shocked!

However, this strange birthday story took a turn toward happiness when Dad's furrowed brow began to give way to a grin. He squeezed my mom's hand and looked a little off into the distance as if remembering the very moment. Then he looked right at me and said, "I met your mother in Kansas City, at TWA, where she was the chief chemist, the youngest in the country. It was wartime and I was working on a plan to speed up aircraft engine cleaning. I had to fly out and work with her on improving the cleaning solutions the military was using. I'll never forget the day I first saw her."

Still holding her hand, Dad turned and looked at Mom, and I felt a rush of warmth and security as I watched my parents gaze lovingly into each other's eyes.

"I refused to marry him," Mom said as she took over their tale. "He was a brash, cocky, and arrogant man from California, and I was from solid Midwestern stock. Who did he think he was, coming to Missouri and trying to whisk me away to a state with no morals? To *California* of all places!!"

"But I knew I was going to marry her anyway," said Dad, still smiling. "She was the oldest of five in her family, told me she loved children and wanted to have a dozen. I spent time with her family, and as I watched her with her younger brothers, I admired her tenderness and patience. She was everything I ever wanted, but your mother made me work hard to convince her. I courted her, flew her out to California to meet my friends, went to church, and did everything I could. I sent her a dozen long-stemmed red roses every week for four years, until it finally seemed that nothing would ever work.

"Until the letter…," my Mom smiled. They exchanged that syrupy sweet look again and I, as a seven-year-old, let out a giggle. "I sent your mother a letter that told her how much I loved her and she finally said 'Yes!'" Dad added. "We honeymooned in San Francisco. I bought her a fresh gardenia corsage from an old street vendor and paraded down Market Street with your mother on my arm. No man was ever happier and no woman was ever more beautiful."

I knew the rest of the story. Over the years Mom and Dad planned for their dozen children and my friends were jealous that I, as the oldest, always seemed to have a new baby to cuddle. Seven times I opened my arms and my heart to a new live baby doll who would look up at me, laugh with me, and love me.

One day in recent years, I took out a box of old family pictures my mother had let me borrow. There I was with all those babies. In the midst of the unsorted pictures was a big photo of my mom and dad strolling down a street in

Letters—
Often love letters convey the
message of our heart without
letting words get in the way

San Francisco. Mom had on what I knew to be her honeymoon suit, with the big brimmed hat. Dad was so proud of her as she clutched onto his arm. Clipped onto the photo was an envelope. I took the proposal letter and as I unfolded it carefully, I wondered if it was all right for me to read it. I had never known what the letter said. I assumed it was some deep, passionate and poetic profession of undying love. It was that, all right, but in the sweet simplicity of my dad's handwriting, these are the words that filled the front and back of four pages. Simple words that had won my mother's heart:

Dear Miss Riley,

I love you. . .

All my love,

Rowland

Our letters don't always have to be perfect or profound— just filled with love. If four years of red roses haven't worked, try the simple words, "I love you."

WRITTEN BY ROWLAND SWEET TO MISS RILEY (SWEET)
SUBMITTED BY ROSE SWEET

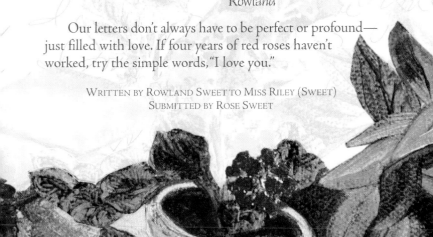

Letters in the Time of Absence

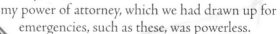

*M*y husband is in the United States Navy, so as you can well imagine we have gone through trials of separation. Although quite often expected, you're usually never prepared.

There was one separation that I definitely wasn't prepared for. It took its toll from the first day my husband departed and went downhill from there. I remember seeing him off at the airport and then leaving from there to have pictures made of our 7-month and 22-month old. I thought this would make a nice gift to send him for Father's Day, which he would not be home for. Matthew and Ashlee were each dressed in matching his and hers bright white sailor suits trimmed in red and blue. During the photo shoot Matthew cut his thumb wide open on a metal pipe. One of God's finest Florence Nightingales happened by and drove us to the hospital where Matthew received 14 stitches to his little chubby thumb.

I didn't realize it then but this was a precursor to what was to take place over the next four months of separation. During that time I was in a terrible car accident and totaled our one and only car. I battled with the insurance company for weeks awaiting new transportation. No transportation with two little ones is agonizing enough, but then came the process of buying a car. Unfortunately, my career as a mother labeled me as gainfully unemployed relying fully on my husband's salary, and he wasn't available for verification. Even my power of attorney, which we had drawn up for emergencies, such as these, was powerless.

> *When I go to the mailbox each day and rifle through reams of ads and flyers, my heart always unconsciously seeks the handwritten return address of a friend.*
>
> —ALEXANDRA STODDARD

From there we went from chronic illness to the death of the family cat and so on. Need I say more?

My best friend, the one I put so much faith in to see me through when I was exhausted at the end of the day from being mom, wasn't there to offer a hand. The one and only thing that I could gain the support from were his letters. Oh how I longed for those letters!

Things are different in the Navy these days. Now we have cell phones, emails, and instant messaging. And although we are so high tech with all of our gidgets and gadgets, they still can't offer the one thing that a handwritten letter has to offer, and that is the personal touch that conveys through the handwritten letter to the one you love.

Are you absent from someone you love? Why not write them a letter and fill their silver mailbox with thoughts from you?

SUBMITTED BY TAMMY BENNETT

Letters—
Your mailbox is your only companion when distance comes between you and your true love

My Silver Mailbox

While she endured the lonely days and nights as a military
wife, Tammy penned heartfelt poetry to her husband.

I silently weep because you're not here.

I've taken such comfort in our friendship of old.

My days are long and the nights are short
as I dream of my friend.

But alas tomorrow is yet another day.

To get through this day is an act of desperation
without my friend.

But I know I must rely on God now and Him alone.

He knows my pain and numbs the empty void I feel
when I think of you.

I've just about made it through another day
when it's time to take my key to the silver box.

I turn the key with anticipation and the box slowly opens
to reveal my treasures.

I quickly remove them for they are very private.

I keep them concealed the best that I can
until I am safely back at my doorstep.

Slowly, one by one, I examine each one
with an inquisitive eye.

I thumb through each one knowing that sooner or later
they will each have to be addressed.

But not now, because there in the midst of each one
that wants to take, I find the one that wants to give.

It's a letter from you.

My heart draws a deep breath
as I gently open the embossed envelope.

There concealed within the envelope is delicate linen stationary
waiting to unfold your words.

Expectantly, I unfold the letter knowing that your words
will be like medicine to my spirit.

I read over them and over them again
not wanting to miss one word.

And then, I methodically stow them away
in a secret place that only I know.

I go to that secret place often just to revisit the old letters.

I know their words haven't changed but often their effect has.

You see, often I can read between the lines
and feel comforted by all the things you didn't write.

I wait now to visit my silver mailbox again and again
until it finally brings news of your return.

Because as much as I long for your letters, I long for you more.

TAMMY BENNETT

Cards and Letters to Be Cherished

Birthdays are particularly precious to me because I lost my mother at an early age to breast cancer. Being a breast cancer survivor myself, I hold memories dear to my heart through cards and letters I receive from members of my family. They unknowingly reached out to me then and are still reaching out to me every time I reread the words that they penned years before. These three are among my favorites, and they all arrived for my 46th birthday on February 21, 1997.

Dear Mommy,

We love you to pieces! You are the best, radical Mommy! Happy, Happy Birthday!

Love,

Megan (age 10) and Julia (age 5)

Dear Mom,

Happy (what is it, 46th?) Birthday! You're so young! For reals, you have no evident wrinkles, you have cute stylin' hair and are pure fun to be with! Sometimes I'd rather hang out with you than kids my age. You are my best friend.

All My Love,

Trisha Lynn (age 20)

Forty-six years ago, while my dad was out mowing the lawn, my mom suddenly realized that I was about to be born. Having no time to get her to the hospital, my dad ran the two blocks to the doctor's office and yelled, "The baby's coming out!" The doctor made it in time for me to land on newsprint, in my parents' bed. The doctor in his haste forgot his bag and sent my dad to once again run the two blocks. Dad missed the whole thing! Huffing and puffing, he got back in time to see the doctor hold me up in a diaper and pronounce my "official" weight, "Oh, about eight pounds!"

From my Dad, Tony Beltman, Stephensville, Texas:

Congratulations Sheri!

I am thinking about you today and what a splash you made when you arrived on the scene 46 years ago. There's no doubt your birthday stands out in my memory as one "tumultuous" day. I had to look in the dictionary as to how to spell that word. Its meaning almost blew me away: agitation, bluster, bustle, commotion, confusion, disorder, disturbance, ferment, flurry, hubbub, hurly-burly, noise, outbreak, racket, riot, turbulence, turmoil, and uproar. Yep, that's the kind of day it was.

Save your special cards and letters to reread over and over again. I'm so glad I saved mine. Whenever I'm feeling blue, all I have to do is read one of these notes from the past. They chase the frowns away and replace them with smiles for the day.

SUBMITTED BY SHERI MULDER

Letters—
Birthday greetings are more than just a celebration of another year of life, they are a reflection of the lives you have blessed

Jeremy's Lunchbox Letters

*O*ne evening on my way to a parent-teacher conference, I prepared myself to hear what antics my red-haired son had done this year. To my surprise, his fifth-grade teacher didn't want to talk about his comical misbehavior. She wanted to talk about lunchtime.

Every morning as I packed my son Jeremy's lunch, I put notes in his lunchbox, sometimes cutting letters and words out of magazines to make a collage, or other times drawing a maze or puzzle of words he would have to decipher. Occasionally, I created a pictorial scene out of construction paper, like a cat sitting on a wooden fence looking at the moon. I spent more time on seasonal notes to make holidays special. It was just part of making lunch.

The teacher wanted to thank me for the notes I put in his lunchbox.

I had no idea what seemed common to me was actually unusual. Unbelievably, no other parent spent time writing notes each day. She said, "The class can't wait to see what Jeremy has in his lunchbox, and they read what you write him." Jeremy loved the attention and took it for granted, never telling me that my private gesture of love had become a daily show-and-tell for the fifth-grade class!

Letters—
Encouraging words nourish
our spirit, just as food
nourishes our body

Years later after Jeremy was grown, I saw his fifth-grade teacher again. She told me with tears in her eyes that she tells the story of Jeremy's lunchbox letters to her classes every year. "I never will forget seeing all the children gather round at lunch each day to read those letters. You wrote those letters to Jeremy but every child received a blessing and wished his mother wrote him notes." She put her arms around my shoulders and continued, "In all my years of teaching, you are the only parent who ministered to me along with the children. Thank you."

Have you ever thought of tucking a note in a lunchbox? What about packing a letter in an overnight bag? There are so many ways we can express our thoughts to our loved ones with just a Post-it and a pen. Be creative! It really takes so little sometimes to be a big blessing. Do you know someone who needs your words of encouragement today?

SUBMITTED BY LUCY MCGUIRE

Letters—
God knew you would need special words to
brighten your day, long before the Pony
Express was a new idea

Surprise Package

About eight years ago, our church surprised my pastor-husband for Christmas with an overwhelming present. He opened a large box on Christmas morning and discovered it was filled with letters from the congregation expressing their appreciation and love for him. They listed specific ways his sermons or Sunday School lessons had helped them. They remembered hospital visits, prayers, and physical help he'd given their families. They also reminded him of the times he moved furniture, baby-sat their children, worked in their yards with them, or even helped put out fires when he was on the volunteer fire department. Letters from officers of the church, lay leaders, staff, and even children (who said they used to think he was God) brought him to tears. There was even a letter from a Jewish woman who didn't attend our church, but he had visited her when she was in the hospital. He prayed for her just as he does with every patient before leaving the room. She was very sick, and she wrote, "When you said, 'In Jesus Name, Amen' my pain left me. I was healed. I felt it." We sat on the floor and read those letters for a long time Christmas morning. Needless to say, we saved them all and take out a few to reread each Christmas morning as a reminder of this special gift.

SUBMITTED BY LUCY McGUIRE

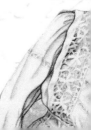

A Lifetime of Letters

*I*n the early years of the twentieth century, it was considered a part of a young girl's training to learn how to write a proper thank-you note. As a part of social graces, each girl was groomed to have polite manners, sit properly, embroider pillowcases, and write thank-you notes on the correct paper with a proper pen.

From the time she was a little girl, Mary Colquitt wrote notes to relatives thanking them for gifts. It became a natural way of life for Mary to be grateful for all favors and to express her appreciation in writing. Throughout her lifetime, she continued this practice sending off everything from two-line notes to lengthy epistles to her parents, her husband, her children and grandchildren, her relatives, her friends, and various church ministers along the way. There was never a suggestion that people save these letters, but many did.

When Mary died in 1994 after 57 years of marriage, many of the grieving friends mentioned specific letters she had written that came at a point in their lives when they needed a word of encouragement. The one memory that united young and old was Mary's love for people as expressed through her offering of gracious words.

Letters—

The blessing of a letter to the one who receives it, brings joy to the soul of the one who sent it. The more you send the more you receive

> *Take away the art of writing from this world,*
> *and you will probably take away its glory.*

> —*LES NATCHEZ*

As her family learned of her constant letter writing, they decided to see how many of these epistles they could collect and put into a scrapbook. Their request went out and her handwritten souvenirs came in. Starting with a letter she had written on her honeymoon in 1939, ranging to a love letter she had written her husband six days before her death, the collection included 400 letters and spanned more than 50 years of care and concern for others. Her daughters put these pages together and had them published in January 1995.

As I learned about Mary's gift of letter writing, I wondered how many people have saved my letters. Would there be enough words for a book?

SUBMITTED BY APRIL JOHNSON

U.S. POSTAGE
6c

FRANKLIN D. ROOSEVELT

Letters from FDR

Although his paralyzed feet hung limply from his legs, Franklin Delano Roosevelt's hands penned some of the most powerful letters in history. His letters to Winston Churchill and their friendship that was forged on stationery, touched millions of lives and helped to change the world. Some of his letters were simple words of encouragement to polio patients, and one particularly powerful letter encouraged heartsick soldiers during the war.

Roosevelt, a consummate letter writer, corresponded not only with his political pen, but also with one that gave hope to millions of polio victims around the world. When he spent time working out in the mineral pools at Warm Springs, Georgia, FDR received hundreds of letters from others afflicted with the illness. Many polio patients received personally written replies from their future president.

FDR went on to become governor of New York and in 1932 was elected president of the United States, his first of four terms. During the latter part of his presidency, Hitler inaugurated the Second World War by unleashing the German Army in Poland. Roosevelt wanted to establish a strong contact

Letters —
The influence of the pen reaches beyond the
influence of mortal man when mortal man
reaches beyond himself to inspire others

> *My pens are symbols of endless possibilities.*
> *They are an extension of myself.*
>
> —ALEXANDRA STODDARD

with a British leader who might eventually become Prime Minister so he wrote a brief note to Britain's First Lord of the Admiralty, Winston Churchill. In his first letter, FDR's easy writing style foreshadowed the life-long friendship that was to follow. He built upon their common naval experiences and their love of history. Churchill responded with alacrity and mild humor, choosing a transparent code name "Naval Person." A year later Churchill did indeed leave the admiralty and take up residency at number 10 Downing Street as Britain's Prime Minister. From then on, Churchill wryly signed letters to FDR as "Former Naval Person." It was the beginning of a cherished and intimate correspondence unparalleled by national leaders.

One of the simplest letters of encouragement Roosevelt wrote might have been the one inside the cover of a government issue Bible that touched lives most profoundly. When the Japanese bombed Pearl Harbor in 1941, countless of our husbands, fathers, brothers, and sons were trapped in a nightmare of personal fear, pain, deep loneliness, death, and despair. Sometimes letters from home were the only patches of light in an otherwise dark and dreary time. With letters, our soldiers could "feel" arms of loved ones around them no matter where they were. Sometimes, though, it was impossible for letters to get through to these men for months at a time. Those were the darkest hours when their prayers for letters seemed to go unanswered. A friend told me his father's story, like so many others, where he sat huddled in a cold, wet soldier's tent, hungry, exhausted, and despairing of ever returning to life as he knew it back home. "God, would you please send me a letter!" was his silent cry, knowing there was no way that mail could ever work its way to his post. The soldier stuck his hand deep down inside his pack, looking for a cigarette, and pulled out the small, brown book with gold letters. It was government issue, made to fit perfectly inside his uniform pocket, and he'd forgotten about it for these many months in battle. Something made him open the cover, where he found the "letter" that seemed to be written just for him:

March 6, 1941

The White House
Washington

To the Members of the Army,

As Commander in Chief, I take pleasure in commending the reading of the Bible to all who serve in the armed forces of the United States. Throughout the centuries, men of many faiths and diverse origins have found in the Sacred Book words of wisdom, counsel, and inspiration. It is a fountain of strength and now, as always, an aid in attaining the highest aspirations of the human soul.

Very Sincerely Yours,
Franklin Delano Roosevelt
(signature)

Tears came to the soldier's eyes and a warm peace flooded his soul as he flipped through the pages and read, "I will take refuge in the shadow of your wings until the disaster has passed…he sends from heaven and saves me…for great is your love…your faithfulness reaches to the skies." (Psalm 57 NIV)

Finding comfort in Scripture during the war, many men and women rededicated themselves spiritually and were able to return home and fight everyday battles of life; wives who had left, children who had grown, homes that had been lost. Those who returned rooted in God's Word were able to pass the baton of their faith on to the third and fourth generations, where even today the effects of our fathers' and grandfathers' lives are being felt. By his letter of encouragement to the men who fought in World War II, and by directing them to Scripture, the leader of our nation inspired men to seek solace in their Creator, to do as he had, "to think about the fundamentals of living and learn the greatest of all lessons."

SUBMITTED BY ROSE SWEET

The pen is mightier than the sword.
—EDWARD BULWER-LYTTON

My Guardian Angel

*O*ften we think of someone who was a blessing to us in the past, but seldom do we sit down and write that special person a thank-you note. *It's been so long… Perhaps they've forgotten… Would they care?* runs through our minds.

Linda found a picture of herself and her sister when they were children and was reminded of how Jannet had always been her protector. Had she ever thanked her? Linda found some stationery with a guardian angel on it and penned this note to her sister.

November 1, 1998

Dear Jannet,

I found a picture of us dressed in our Easter finery that exemplifies our relationship. You have your arm around me and I'm smiling. I'm shrinking back from the camera into your protective shadow.

You continue to put your arms around my shoulders literally and figuratively. For instance, I don't remember my first day of school being traumatic. Perhaps this is because the first and second grades were in the same classroom and Sister Mary Gabriella let me sit next to you.

Letters—

A letter of thanks is never overdue. Even though seasons pass, lives change, and memories fade, the words of a dear one will go back in time and acknowledge the thank-yous that were once forgotten

I don't know if I ever expressed my appreciation to you before. I know that you kept me out of (serious) trouble. My obvious acceptance of your protection continued through most of our school days. In fact, unless I got obstinate, you kept me out of trouble at home and at school.

Only years later, when we were no longer going to the same high school, did I learn to appreciate how well you watched over me. Suddenly, I felt like a shy clam without a shell. I had to learn the hard lesson of how to begin to function without you on a daily, practical basis.

I didn't grasp how to do this instantly or spontaneously. Thankfully, you continued to protect me during the times you were aware that I needed help. And I did need help the day I got home from getting my tonsils out and answered a business call intended for Mom. I couldn't talk above a raspy whisper. Perhaps the man who called was hard-of-hearing. Or, perhaps he thought I was goofing off. He certainly wasn't a gentleman when he started yelling at me.

What relief to see you walk through the door from your college classes. You arrived just in time to handle an impossible-for-me situation. You plunked your books down on the table as you strode across the kitchen. Hurrah! You brought the bully to his knees when you took the receiver from my shaking hand and barked into the phone, "WHAT DO YOU WANT?" It sounded more like a command than a question.

Although our relationship is tempered by years, distance, and circumstances, maybe big sisters never completely grow out of their protective role. I know that I'm blessed with having you for an older sister. And I'm grateful that you were my earthly guardian angel during my growing-up years.

Hug,

Linda

Jannet was surprised and touched to see that her "little sister" still remembered her years of being the earthly guardian angel.

Is there someone who cared for you years ago? Would a belated thank-you note still be a blessing?

SUBMITTED BY LINDA LAMAR JEWELL
WRITTEN BY FLORENCE LITTAUER

Letters—
Often express deep emotions
that go unsaid

This is my letter to the world,
that never wrote to me.

—EMILY DICKINSON